Engineers

Richard Tames

Chrysalis Children's Books

First published in the UK in 2003 by
Chrysalis Children's Books
64 Brewery Road, London N7 9NT
Copyright © Chrysalis Books PLC 2003
Text by Richard Tames

ISBN 1 84138 723 1
British Library Cataloguing in Publication Data for this book is available from the British Library.

A Belitha Book
Managing Editor: Joyce Bentley
Assistant Editor: Clare Chambers
Editor: Rosalind Beckman
Designer: Sarah Crouch
Picture Researcher: Jenny Barlow

J620
1454434

Printed in Hong Kong
10 9 8 7 6 5 4 3 2 1

Picture credits:
B = bottom; L = left; R = right; T = top.
Cover front and back (bridge) Rex (Brunel) Hulton Archive 4 T Ancient Art & Architecture Collection B Mary Evans 5 Corbis/Chinch Gryniewicz/Ecoscene 6 The Art Archive/Ephesus Museum Turkey/Dagli Orti (A) 7 T Corbis B The Art Archive/Dagli Orti (A) 8 Science Museum/SSPL 9 T Corbis B The Art Archive/Topkapi Museum Istanbul/Dagli Orti 10 Hulton Archive 11 T The Art Archive/Musée du Louvre Paris/Dagli Orti (A) B Science Museum/SSPL 12 Corbis/Ted Spiegel 13 T The Art Archive/Manoir du Clos Lucé /Dagli Orti B Science Museum/SSPL 14 Science Museum/SSPL 15 T Mary Evans B Science Museum/SSPL 16 The Art Archive 17 T Hulton Archive B By courtesy of The National Portrait Gallery, London 18 Hulton Archive 19 B Mary Evans 20 Rex/Timepix/Fritz Goro 21 T The Art Archive/Gunshots B Hulton Archive 22 Mary Evans/Institution of Civil Engineers 23 T Corbis/Michael Freeman B The Art Archive/ The Parker Gallery London/Harper Collins Publishers 24 Hulton Archive 25 T Hulton Archive B Science Museum/SSPL 26 T National Railway Museum/SSPL B Science Museum/SSPL 26-27 National Railway Museum/SSPL 27 T Corbis/Bettmann B National Railway Museum/SSPL 28 Hulton Archive 28-29 and 29 National Railway Museum/SSPL 30 Hulton Archive 31 Science Museum/SSPL 32 T Rex B Hulton Archive 33 T Hulton Archive B Science Museum/SSPL 34 Hulton Archive 35 T Corbis/Bettmann B Hulton Archive 36 T Corbis/Darrell Gulin B Hulton Archive 37 Corbis/Bettmann 38 and 39 Hulton Archive 40 T Mary Evans B Corbis/Underwood & Underwood 41 The Art Archive/Bibliothèque des Arts Décoratifs Paris/Dagli Orti (A) 42 Rex 43 T Hulton Archive B Philip Jarrett 44 Mary Evans 45 T Mary Evans B Hulton Archive.
All reasonable efforts have been made to trace the relevant copyright holders of the images contained within this book. If we were unable to reach you, please contact Chrysalis Children's Books.

CONTENTS

Introduction   4

Hero of Alexandria   6

Leonardo da Vinci   10

James Watt   14

Eli Whitney   18

Thomas Telford   22

The Stephensons   26

The Brunels   30

Thomas Edison   34

Henry Ford   38

The Wright brothers   42

Glossary   46

Index   48

INTRODUCTION

Since ancient times engineers have designed the world around us. Engineers use science to design and make machines and structures such as bridges, dams, roads, railways and canals.

Ancient skills

The building of Stonehenge nearly 5000 years ago was a triumph of practical engineering skills. The wheel had not yet been invented, but the people who built Stonehenge transported stones weighing up to 4 tons over 380 km from Wales. The designers of the Great Pyramid in Egypt, built over 4000 years ago, were able to make its four sides almost exactly equal. Until the nineteenth century it remained the tallest building in the world.

Simple tools and muscle power were used to build the Great Wall of China.

No need for machinery

The Great Wall of China, stretching over 2250 km, was built by forced labour. Despite producing such useful goods as paper, silk, gunpowder and the compass, the Chinese showed little interest in developing labour-saving machines. The same was true of the Romans, who invented concrete and built superb roads, baths and **aqueducts**. Hero of Alexandria even invented a steam engine, a great labour-saving device, but found no real use for it.

When constructing buildings such as Stonehenge, slave labour had to be well organised to work effectively.

Ideas only

The history of engineering shows that many ideas that were sound in theory often proved impossible to put into practice for lack of the right materials. Leonardo da Vinci made designs for paddle-boats, helicopters and armoured vehicles that were only turned into practical machines centuries after his death.

Learning by doing

Modern engineering was born during the Industrial Revolution of the eighteenth century, which drew on the practical skills of men who made and mended **watermills**, clocks and scientific or **navigational instruments**. Many of the early engineers such as Thomas Telford and George Stephenson had little or no schooling, and were self-taught. Even much later inventors such as Henry Ford and Thomas Edison had no formal training and did not study at university.

Civil and mechanical engineering

Civil engineering deals with the building of roads, railways, bridges and **canals**. **Mechanical engineering** involves making locomotives, ships and other kinds of machinery. The early engineers often had to be masters of both. As a young man in America, Marc Brunel surveyed the route for a canal, set up a weapons factory, made machines for casting and **boring** cannons, and designed harbour defences and a theatre. His son, Isambard, built railways, bridges and steamships.

Specialised skills

From the middle of the nineteenth century civil and mechanical engineering developed into two separate professions. **Marine engineering** – designing engines and equipment for ships – became another separate speciality. During the twentieth century new specialised fields of engineering emerged, such as electrical, **automotive** and aeronautical engineering. Most engineers are now trained at university, but they still have to master the basic skills and methods developed by the pioneers whose stories are told in this book.

The technology developed by today's engineers in factories and research institutes is essential in improving the environment and providing a better standard of living for all.

HERO OF ALEXANDRIA

Lived during the 1st century AD

Around 2000 years ago, Hero, also known as Heron, invented the world's first steam engine. He wrote books about mathematics, but unlike most scientists of the ancient world, he was also interested in solving practical problems.

Hero was a Greek who lived in the Egyptian city of Alexandria. He was mainly interested in mathematics and wrote books about how to measure the surface area of triangles, circles, cones, pyramids, **cylinders** and spheres. He also developed the theory of dividing a circle into 360 degrees. Although mathematics and scientific principles were widely known in the ancient world, Hero was one of the first to use this knowledge to solve practical problems.

Unknown genius

Hero's writings are all technical handbooks; they tell us nothing about Hero himself. Even the years of his birth and death are unknown. We only know that he was alive in 62 AD because he wrote about an **eclipse** of the Sun that astronomers can prove took place that year.

A statue of Hero as a young boy. Hero was a gifted mathematician who wrote books about the air- and steam-powered machines he invented.

A debt to the Arabs

Many of Hero's writings have been lost over the centuries and are known only because other writers have referred to them. Some ancient writings have survived because Muslim scholars understood their value and translated them into Arabic. Later these were translated into Latin so that they could be read in Europe. Hero's own book on how to measure things, *Metrica*, was lost for centuries and only rediscovered in 1896. This picture shows Hero's design for a steam-powered organ.

Roman requirements

It is possible that Hero was interested in applying his knowledge to everyday tasks because during his lifetime Egypt was ruled by the Romans. The Romans admired Greek learning but they were more concerned with protecting their vast empire. For this they needed to build fine roads, strong forts and impressive public buildings such as temples and law courts.

Writing books

Hero probably realised that in order to become well known and attract students, he needed to write about what would be useful as well as interesting. This included how to design weapons of war. He also wrote books about water clocks, how to measure land and how to lift heavy weights.

Problem solver

Hero devised tables of calculations for architects to show how they could safely build large arches, wells and tunnels without danger of collapse, and designed a screw press for squeezing juice from grapes and oil from olives. He was also interested in **astronomy**, mirrors, light and reflection. He opened a technical school that held classes devoted to research and experiments.

The wealth of ancient Alexandria can be seen from the remains of the city's magnificent public buildings.

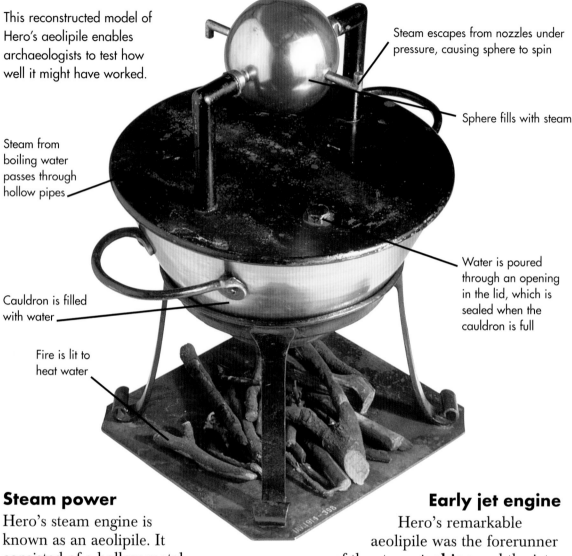

This reconstructed model of Hero's aeolipile enables archaeologists to test how well it might have worked.

Steam escapes from nozzles under pressure, causing sphere to spin

Sphere fills with steam

Steam from boiling water passes through hollow pipes

Water is poured through an opening in the lid, which is sealed when the cauldron is full

Cauldron is filled with water

Fire is lit to heat water

Steam power

Hero's steam engine is known as an aeolipile. It consisted of a hollow metal sphere, like a balloon, that was connected to two pipes. The pipes stood in a boiler (rather like a cauldron with a lid on top) that was filled with water. At the top and bottom of the sphere were bent nozzles. When the water in the boiler was heated, the steam passed through the pipes into the sphere and came out through the nozzles, making the sphere spin round.

Early jet engine

Hero's remarkable aeolipile was the forerunner of the steam **turbine** and the jet engine, but at the time it had no practical use. In theory, the aeolipile could have been developed to drive machines; in practice, this was never likely to happen in ancient Egypt where slaves were plentiful. Since slaves were given only basic food, clothing and shelter, there was no need for expensive machines to help them with heavy work.

Spectacular inventions

Hero used heated air to open the doors of a temple as if by magic – or by the hands of unseen gods. He also invented a fire engine; two organs – one powered by water and another by a windmill; war catapults; **vending machines** operated by coins pushed through a slot; and a system of **gears** that used 5 kg of force to lift 1000 kg of weight. Another invention was a bowl that mysteriously topped itself up whenever wine was ladled out of it. It was controlled by a hidden **valve** on a pipe that let wine flow in whenever the level went down.

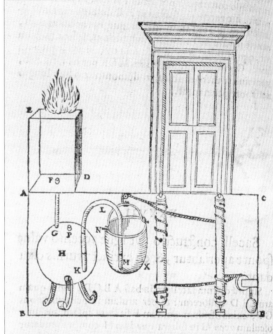

A B C D, Ex cardinibus catenulæ in vnum coactæ per trochleam ad vas N X concauum & fufpenfum religentur; alteræ vero catenulę cardinibus obuolutæ, fuperioribufque contrariæ, & in vnum coactæ per trochleam reli-

The invention of the printing press spread knowledge of the writings of the ancient world. This drawing shows Hero's design for a mechanism that opened doors.

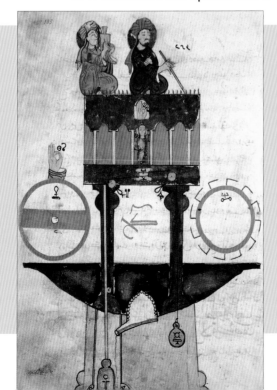

An Alexandrian forerunner

Many of Hero's devices were probably based on ideas first put forward by Ctesibius who, around 270 BC, had also lived in Alexandria. Ctesibius was uneducated, but he was very inventive and was the first person to realise that air under pressure (**pneumatic** power) could be used to operate machines. His inventions included the first accurate water clock, which measured time by the speed with which water flowed out of a vessel. He then added a dial with a pointer and decorative figures that used the flow of the water to make the dial move. This picture shows a Turkish waterclock from the thirteenth century.

LEONARDO DA VINCI

1452–1519

Leonardo was such a talented engineer and inventor that his ideas were far ahead of their time. This made it difficult to turn many of his theories into practice.

Leonardo took his surname from his birthplace, Vinci, near Empoli, a town between Pisa and Florence in Italy. His early education included reading, writing, arithmetic, **geometry** and Latin, which was still an international language used throughout Europe. From the age of 14, Leonardo trained as a painter in the Italian city of Florence. His teacher was Andrea del Verrocchio, who was a **sculptor** and goldsmith as well as a painter.

A man of many talents

Leonardo taught himself the new art of painting with oil-based paints, which had been invented in the Netherlands. His earliest known drawings include sketches of machines, ranging from pumps to weapons of war. In his thirst for knowledge, he became interested in subjects as varied as **botany** and town planning.

Many of Leonardo's ideas were developed during the last century and now are used every day throughout the world.

World-famous artist

Leonardo is best known for his art. He left many drawings and sketches but only 17 paintings, some of which are unfinished. His paintings are some of the most famous in the world – *The Last Supper* and the *Mona Lisa* (above). Leonardo wrote that 'Painting is a science and all sciences are based on mathematics.'

The favour of the Duke

When he was 30, Leonardo was hired by the Duke of Milan to be his artist and engineer. Leonardo had written to him, explaining his ideas for warfare: 'I know how to make . . . bridges . . . covered chariots . . . big guns . . . catapults and other machines.' He produced paintings and statues for the Duke, designed the scenery and costumes for festivals and advised on buildings and **fortifications**. During the 1490s, Leonardo made a detailed study to show how complicated machines are made up of basic devices such as the pulley, the **axle** and the **lever**. His drawings included different kinds of springs, chains, toothed wheels and ball bearings.

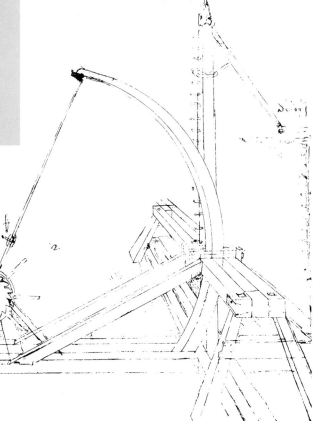

Leonardo's designs for war machines like this catapult show that when various simple mechanical devices are put together, human muscle power can be greatly increased.

A lost masterpiece

Leonardo spent 12 years working on a huge statue (5m high) of one of the Duke's ancestors on horseback, but when the time came to **cast** it, the metal was used to make cannon because a war had broken out. The full-size clay model he made was shot to pieces by French soldiers, who used it for target practice.

Back to Florence

In 1502 Leonardo worked for the soldier, Cesare Borgia, commander of the Pope's army, drawing maps and designing fortifications for him. In 1503, he devised a way of diverting the River Arno so that the people of Pisa, an enemy of Florence, would be cut off from the sea. When he returned to Florence, he surveyed a route for a canal that would join the city to the sea. Today, a motorway follows exactly the route that he had suggested.

Theories on paper

Like so many of Leonardo's brilliant ideas, these schemes were recorded in notebooks but were never carried out. Leonardo also continued with his scientific studies – dissecting bodies to improve his knowledge of **anatomy**, and making notes on the flight of birds and how water flowed in currents.

Moving on

From 1506 to 1513 Leonardo lived in Milan, which had been captured by the French. He designed a canal to link the city with Lake Como but it remained another project that was never completed. He settled in France for the last years of his life. Working for the French King, Francis I, he designed a palace and a garden, and a mechanical lion to amuse people at the King's coronation.

Valuable notebooks

Leonardo planned to write books about painting, **architecture**, machinery and anatomy. These were never completed but he filled over 40 notebooks with thousands of pages of ideas and drawings. After his death some of his notebooks were stored away; others were lost. Leonardo remained famous as an artist but his interest in science was only rediscovered when his notebooks were found in the twentieth century.

This official document signed by Cesare Borgia confirms Leonardo's appointment as senior military architect and general engineer.

Leonardo's sketch for a man-powered helicopter, based on a screw-shaped spiral. The wings were to be made of starched linen. Over 5000 pages of notes and sketches have been discovered.

Machines for a modern age

Leonardo sketched plans for inventions that were only made successfully hundreds of years after his death. These include the helicopter, tank, machine-gun, parachute, paddle-boat and underwater breathing apparatus. He also drew up plans for machines to make mirrors, ropes, files and screws, and for useful devices such as a calculator, a dredging machine and a revolving crane. Although very few of his inventions developed beyond the stage of a sketch or at most a working model, Leonardo was undoubtedly a genius, centuries ahead of his time.

A brilliant man

In 1550 Giorgio Vasari wrote a biography of Leonardo and explained why he had achieved so little in practice. 'It is clear that Leonardo, through his understanding of art, began many things and never finished them, because it seemed to him that the human hand could not perfectly carry out the things he imagined because his ideas were so clever and so marvellous.'

Mirror writing

Leonardo was left-handed and deliberately wrote his notes from right to left and the wrong way round. He also used a special kind of shorthand that he invented himself. This made it very difficult for people to read his notes and steal his ideas.

JAMES WATT

1736–1819

Although the steam engine was invented before Watt was born, his improved design revolutionised the manufacture of goods in Britain. Thanks to his partnership with a brilliant businessman, he benefited financially from his own inventions and became a wealthy man.

The son of a joiner, James Watt was born in Greenock, Scotland. While still a boy he was given his own workbench, where he made models of cranes and barrel organs. His ambition was to manufacture scientific instruments and he learned his trade in Glasgow and London. By the age of 21 he was making instruments for the science and maths teachers at Glasgow University.

Breakthrough in steam

Although the first steam engine was patented by Thomas Savery in 1698, a more practical and powerful machine was invented by Thomas Newcomen in 1712. When Watt was asked to repair a small model of a Newcomen engine, he saw that it could work using less fuel. Watt made a working model of his improved engine in 1765 and took out a **patent** to protect his invention in 1769.

Watt was one of many Scotsmen attracted to the new industrial areas of Britain by the need for their technical skills.

In its day, Boulton's Soho Manufactury employed about 1000 workers and was the most famous factory in Europe.

Lack of money

Unfortunately, Watt had no money to manufacture engines for sale. Between 1767 and 1774 he made his living as a **surveyor**, laying out routes for new canals, in particular the Caledonian Canal. A partnership in 1769 with the manufacturer John Roebuck to build a steam engine failed when Roebuck went bankrupt.

Successful partnership

In 1775 Watt went into business with Matthew Boulton, a Birmingham manufacturer of metal goods. Boulton was a clever businessman and had both the money and the factory to make engines. Watt disliked dealing with money problems and his partnership with Boulton left Watt free to focus on engineering without financial worries. He made further improvements to his engine, which meant that it only used a third as much fuel as a Newcomen engine. Boulton and Watt made large profits from the sale of their engines. They also received extra payments because of the fuel they saved.

Reduced fuel costs

The Newcomen engine was used mainly in coal mines where fuel was easy to come by. But in the tin mines of Cornwall, where coal was bought in at great cost, the Boulton and Watt engine was a huge success because fuel bills were cut by two-thirds. When the first Watt engine was installed in Cornwall in 1777, there were 75 Newcomen engines in use in the Cornish mines. By 1783 only one was still in use.

Rotary versus pumps power

The Newcomen and early Watt engines produced a to-and-fro motion, which was only suitable for driving pumps. In 1782 Watt invented a new system of gears that converted the movement to a **rotary** motion so that steam power could be used to drive machines. This meant that industries no longer needed to rely on the power of muscles, wind or water. Rotary engines made the invention of the locomotive possible, but Watt opposed the development of engines for this purpose because he thought they would be too dangerous.

A dramatic improvement

Engines with rotary power were soon installed in two of London's largest factories – the Albion Flour Mills and Whitbread's **Brewery**. In 1814 London's *Times* newspaper became the first in the world to be printed on a steam-powered press. It printed 1100 sheets an hour, which was four times faster than the best hand-operated press.

By the time of Watt's death, steam-powered machinery had revolutionised the manufacture of cotton cloth.

Measuring power

Watt invented a method of measuring the energy generated by his engines and called it 'horsepower'. He estimated that the average horse could lift a weight of 51 kg to a height of 60m in one minute and carry on doing so for an entire working **shift**. Later, scientists devised a unit of energy called a 'watt', named after James Watt. One horsepower is equal to 745.7 watts.

A refusal to retire

In 1785 Watt was elected Fellow of the Royal Society. He retired from business in 1800. By then, the firm of Boulton and Watt had made and installed over 500 engines. Watt remained busy during his retirement. He invented a machine that could copy statues and another that copied letters and drawings. He worked on his inventions until his death in 1819.

A Watt engine.

The Lunar Society

Watt enjoyed the friendship of learned men and was a member of the Lunar Society of Birmingham, which met to discuss science. The society was so-called because it met on the night of the full moon so that members could see their way on their return home. This picture of famous members of the Lunar Society includes some of the people mentioned in this book.

1 Marc Brunel, 2 Matthew Boulton, 3 James Watt, 4 Thomas Telford

ELI WHITNEY

1765–1825

Most famous for his invention of the cotton gin, Eli Whitney was also a pioneer of mass production. His system of interchangeable parts for weapons laid the foundation for modern manufacturing methods.

Eli Whitney was the son of a Massachusetts farmer in the USA. By the time he was 15 he had already set up a workshop for making nails. His family could not afford to send him to university so he worked as a teacher to earn money for his studies. When he was 23, he became a student at Yale University. He attended science lectures but he trained to become a lawyer.

Cotton trade

Whitney settled in Georgia, which was becoming rich from growing cotton for sale to England. The more cotton that could be grown, the larger the profits. The variety of cotton that grew near the coast had its seeds removed by passing it through **rollers**. The different type of cotton that grew in the larger interior regions of the USA was not so easily cleaned as the seeds stuck to the **fibres**.

Eli Whitney set out to become a lawyer rather than an inventor. He found out that the law would prove powerless to protect his invention.

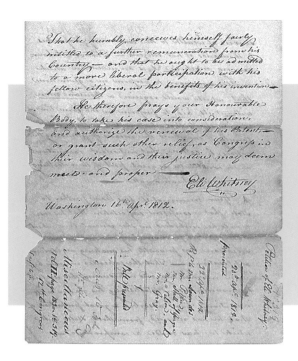

Patent protection

A patent is a legal document giving an inventor the sole right to profit from his or her invention for a fixed number of years. Anyone who wants to use it must pay the inventor for doing so. The first patents were drawn up in England in 1624; they were adopted into US law in 1790. In this letter, written in 1812, Whitney asks for his cotton gin patent to be renewed and better protected.

Efficient cotton gin

Whitney saw that a machine that could remove these sticky seeds would make both America and the inventor rich. It is said that the idea for his invention came to him while watching cows lick stalks of corn with their rough tongues. He made the first version in just ten days. His cotton gin ('gin' is short for engine) was a device that used cylinders set with hooks and **bristles** to strip out the seeds. It was operated by hand and could clean about 23 kg of cotton a day – about 50 times the amount a slave could process. Large-cotton gins, powered by horses or water, could turn out five times as much cotton as a hand-cranked machine.

A small cotton gin was so compact that it could be carried easily to wherever it was needed.

Copied invention

In 1794 Whitney took out a patent for his cotton gin. Unfortunately for him, the gin was very easy for a country blacksmith to build, and cotton farmers had their own made rather than buy from the company Whitney set up. Although Whitney was a lawyer, it was impossible to take every offender to court to enforce his patent and by 1797 he was out of business.

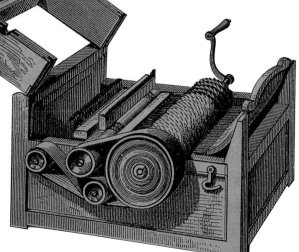

Reaching an agreement

Eventually, a number of states in which cotton was a major crop agreed to pay for the use of the cotton gin. However, most of the money that he received was used to pay off legal costs. Whitney later invented other devices, including a **milling machine**, but after his failure to defend his rights over the cotton gin he decided not to take out a patent.

Fear of war

Between 1798 and 1800 there were a number of conflicts at sea between the USA and France. Afraid that they might develop into open warfare, the US government decided to strengthen its military power. At that time, there were only two government **armouries** in the USA, which had taken three years to produce 1000 **muskets**. Each musket was put together by a skilled craftsman; if a part broke, a replacement had to be made specially. Skilled craftsmen were in short supply in the USA, partly because farming land was cheap or even free. Many young men became farmers rather than spending years training to master a difficult trade.

Muskets in demand

The government wanted 40 000 muskets and asked private companies to supply them. Twenty-six firms put in offers to make a total of 30 200. Whitney offered to make 10 000 in two years. His plan was to design machines that would enable unskilled men to make identical parts that could be fitted together easily.

Whitney first worked on perfecting his cotton gin in a simple shack on a plantation in Georgia.

Whitney's vision

'The tools which I contemplate to make are similar to an engraving on copper plate from which may be taken a great number of impressions.' But instead of producing identical pictures, Whitney would produce identical and, therefore, **interchangeable** parts. If any part broke, it could be replaced easily. Whitney's claim that he could deliver such a huge number of muskets sounded incredible to many people. The sum of $134 000 was paid for the muskets – the largest amount ever paid in a single business deal in the country's history until then. But the government had faith in Whitney – after all, he was the man who had invented the cotton gin.

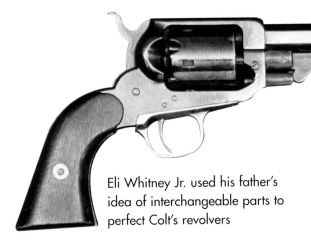

Eli Whitney Jr. used his father's idea of interchangeable parts to perfect Colt's revolvers

Early mass production

In early 1801 Whitney went to Washington DC to meet government officials. He put the different musket parts in separate piles on a table and, taking one at random from each pile, demonstrated how the parts easily fitted together to make a complete musket. In 1811 Whitney took a new order for a further 15 000 muskets and delivered them within two years. This time Whitney made a fortune and kept it.

From muskets to revolvers

After his death, Whitney's weapons factory passed to his only son, Eli Whitney Jr. Whitney Jr. worked closely with Samuel Colt, who designed revolvers. He was given the contract to produce Colt's revolvers, using his father's system of manufacture.

Delay in manufacture

In fact, it took nearly 10 years for Whitney to deliver the 10 000 muskets. At the end of the first year, instead of delivering 4000 as promised, he only delivered 1500. He had problems in obtaining supplies of materials and outbreaks of disease cut back his workforce. Whitney was able to buy more time by demonstrating the value of what he was producing.

Cotton kingdom

Whitney's invention made it profitable to grow cotton on a huge scale in the southern states of the USA. This found a ready market in Britain, where inventors had produced steam-powered machinery for turning cotton into cloth at high speed. However, it is possible that Whitney unwittingly contributed to the continuation of the slave trade. As cotton production increased, many more slaves were needed to work on the **plantations**.

THOMAS TELFORD

1757–1834

Amongst Thomas Telford's many achievements were an improved road network, the development of a canal system and the construction of major bridges. His work in civil engineering made travel and the transportation of goods faster, safer and cheaper.

Thomas Telford, the son of a shepherd, was born in Dumfriesshire in Scotland. He learned the trade of a **stone mason** and taught himself architecture in his spare time. When he became famous, Telford explained that his success was the result of learning the business of building from the bottom up. His career marked the transition from self-taught **amateurs** to trained professionals.

Wider experience

In 1780 Telford moved to Edinburgh. Stone masons were in great demand and Telford worked on buildings in the city's New Town. Two years later, he travelled to London to work on Somerset House, the first ever purpose-built government offices, designed by Sir William Chambers. By 1784 Telford was working in Portsmouth, where he gained experience in constructing harbour walls and docks.

Thomas Telford travelled around Britain to learn new skills and gain experience by working on many different construction projects.

Canals in the air

Telford's most important achievement was to build aqueducts to carry a canal over the Ceiriog and Dee valleys in Wales. The Pont Cysylltau aqueduct was the longest and highest in Britain – 307m long and 37m high – and stood on 18 stone piers. Its Welsh name means 'connecting bridge'. The final section of the canal, built between 1804 and 1808, provided a new means of cheap transport for Welsh slate quarries.

Shropshire surveyor

In 1786 Telford was appointed official surveyor to the county of Shropshire. Shropshire was an important centre for the booming iron and coal industries, but as an inland county it had no easy access to sea transport.

Improved road travel

Telford's method of road-building was based on the Roman system. The first layer was made of large flat stones that fitted closely together. Then came three layers of stones, each smaller in size than the stones below it. On top of that was a layer of gravel. The pounding of traffic over the road packed it down into a firm, hard-wearing surface. Road travel became faster, more reliable and more comfortable than it had been since the days of the Romans. Coaches drawn by teams of horses could average a steady 12 km/h. Timetables that had once been measured to the nearest hour could now be organised to the minute.

A stage-coach passing through a toll gate at night. Improved roads made round-the-clock travel possible.

Canals expert

Britain's first canals were built to link coal mines to towns. Although canals sometimes dried up in summer and froze in winter, they were much cheaper for transporting bulky goods than hauling them on carts by road. Canals soon found new business carrying grain, timber and bricks. The 1790s saw a boom in canal building. In 1793 the Ellesmere Canal Company appointed Telford as its engineer with the task of building a canal to connect the rivers Severn, Dee and Mersey. Telford also built a canal from Wolverhampton to Nantwich in Cheshire, as well as St Katherine's Dock in London.

Huge project

Telford's greatest project was the Caledonian Canal, which was begun in 1804 and completed in 1822. This required the construction of canals to join up existing natural **lochs** so that boats could pass from south-east to north-west Scotland over a distance of 192 km. The project also involved harbour works at Aberdeen, Leith, Banff, Peterhead and Dundee, 1450 km of link roads and 120 bridges.

Swedish canal

On the same gigantic scale was the construction of the Gota Canal in Sweden to link the North Sea with the Baltic. This project started in 1808 and was completed in 1832. Like the Caledonian Canal, it involved building artificial waterways to join up a chain of natural lakes, making an overall waterway 200 km long.

Shipping canals not only saved time by shortening routes, they also saved ships from the risk of storms at sea.

Two bridges

Telford's suspension bridge (above) was the first bridge to be built across the Menai Strait. At the time, it was the longest suspension bridge ever built. Between 1845 and 1850, Robert Stephenson built a railway bridge within sight of Telford's suspension bridge. Known as the Britannia Bridge (right), it was damaged by fire in 1970 but rebuilt to carry road and rail.

Suspension bridges

Telford developed a special interest in bridges. His biggest bridge spanned the Menai Strait, which divides the island of Anglesey from mainland Wales. A **suspension bridge** made of wrought iron links, the Menai Bridge took from 1819 to 1826 to build and had a finished span of 176m. It reduced the journey time between Holyhead in Anglesey and London by nine hours. Telford built a similar suspension bridge over the Conwy **estuary,** which opened a few months after the Menai Bridge

Honoured by his fellows

Telford was chosen by his fellow engineers to serve as the first President of the Institution of Civil Engineers, which was founded in 1818. It was the first **professional** engineering institution in the world. Its foundation demonstrated that building roads, bridges and canals was a skilled business for trained professionals. Telford was buried in Westminster Abbey. In 1963 the new town of Telford in Shropshire was named in his honour.

THE STEPHENSONS

George Stephenson (1781–1848)
Robert Stephenson (1803–1859)

Father-and-son team, George and Robert Stephenson, worked together to bring railways to the world. George also invented a miner's lamp and Robert built major bridges.

George Stephenson was born in the mining village of Wylam, near the great industrial city of Newcastle upon Tyne, in the north-east of England. His family was too poor to send him to school so he started work at the Killingworth Colliery when he was eight. After work he went to night school, where he learned to read and write.

Talented engineer

George had a talent for mending and inventing machines, which was encouraged by the colliery owners, and eventually became the resident engineer. He built his first locomotive for the colliery. In 1825 he completed the first ever railway for hauling freight between the towns of Stockton and Darlington.

George Stephenson (top) and his son Robert both grew up near Newcastle upon Tyne.

The first locomotive

Railways with horse-drawn carriages for hauling coal existed long before George Stephenson was born. A Cornish mining engineer, Richard Trevithick (1771–1833), invented the first practical locomotive in 1804, which he called *Catch Me Who Can*. Trevithick took it to London to show it off in public in the hope of raising money to make an even better engine, but he was unsuccessful. Instead, he went to South America where he made, and then lost, his fortune.

The Liverpool and Manchester

In 1830 George Stephenson completed the first railway for both freight and passengers, between the booming port of Liverpool and the city of Manchester, home of the cotton industry. He also supplied the locomotives for the railway after winning a competition held at Rainhill in 1829. There, George Stephenson took the controls of *Rocket*, which had been built by his son, Robert. It reached a speed of 30 km/h and easily beat the other competitors. The Liverpool and Manchester line was much busier than the Stockton and Darlington line, with five locomotives, rather than only one. Half a million passengers travelled on it in its first year.

(Above) The Stephensons' *Rocket*.
(Below) Rich people travelled comfortably in covered carriages on the Liverpool and Manchester line. Compare this picture with the one on the next page, which shows how the poorer people travelled.

A modest man

Although he became rich enough to retire, George Stephenson continued to advise on the construction of new lines throughout England and in Belgium, where the first railways on mainland Europe were built. At the age of 64 he laid out the route for a line from Madrid to the coast of Spain. The year before his death he founded the Institution of Mechanical Engineers. George Stephenson was a modest man, who never forgot his humble origins, despite becoming one of the most important men in industrial Britain.

Young worker

George Stephenson put his only child, Robert, in charge of the world's first factory for making locomotives while still only a teenager. Better educated than his father, Robert had already been to an academy in Newcastle and spent some months at university in Edinburgh. In 1824 he went to South America to learn about mining. There he met a penniless Richard Trevithick and gave him money to come home. At 30, Robert was appointed chief engineer of the London to Birmingham line, which was completed in 1838.

Standard gauge

George Stephenson decided that the distance between the two lines of rail should be fixed at 4 ft 8½ in (1.4m). This became the 'standard gauge' used throughout Britain and in many other countries where British engineers built railways. No one is quite sure how Stephenson arrived at this figure. Some people said he simply measured dozens of carts that were in general use in the north-east of England and took the average; others thought it was the width of the **wagonway** at Killingworth Colliery, where Stephenson built his first locomotive.

Royal occasion

In 1849 Queen Victoria came to Newcastle to open the High Level Bridge that Robert Stephenson had designed to carry the railway across the River Tyne. Robert had already built a bridge over the River Tweed at Berwick. The High Level at Newcastle completed the rail link between London and Edinburgh.

Buried with honour

Robert also built a bridge over the River Nile in Egypt and a huge one over the St. Lawrence River at Montreal in Canada. For many years this was the longest bridge in the world. Robert Stephenson never enjoyed good health and he died, aged 56, less than a month after his friend and professional rival, Isambard Kingdom Brunel. He was buried in Westminster Abbey next to the greatest in the land – and right beside the grave of Thomas Telford.

The High Level Bridge was designed to carry three railway tracks on the upper level, with a roadway underneath. It is still in use today.

THE BRUNELS

Sir Marc Isambard Brunel 1769–1849
Isambard Kingdom Brunel 1806–1859

The Brunels pushed engineering to new limits to achieve a remarkable series of firsts, on land, by sea, and even under a major river.

Marc Brunel was a French naval officer, who fled from the French Revolution in 1793 and settled in New York as the city's engineer. He improved New York's defences and built a cannon factory and the Bowery Theatre. In 1799 he came to Britain to marry an English girl whom he had met seven years before.

Quick and efficient

During the early 1800s, Britain was expanding its navy for a war with France that would last until 1815. There was a great need for pulley-blocks – wooden rollers that used ropes to raise and lower ships' sails. Brunel designed a set of 43 machines that made pulley-blocks faster and better than they could by hand. Using Brunel's machines, ten men could do the work of a hundred. This was one of the world's first examples of **mass production**, similar to Whitney's system for making muskets. Brunel also made a variety of other machines – for knitting stockings, making boots and sawing and bending wood.

The ambitious engineering projects of Marc Brunel (top) and his son Isambard transformed the lives of people in Britain and throughout the world.

Business problems

In 1814 Brunel's business was damaged by fire. As a result, he and his partners lost a great deal of money. Then, when the war with the French ended in 1815, the British government refused to pay Brunel for army boots it had ordered from him. Brunel continued to work on new projects, building a suspension bridge in France and a floating pier in Liverpool, but he still had financial problems. In 1821 he was imprisoned for debt for a number of months until the government finally paid him the money he was owed.

Marc Brunel's block-making machines were so successful that the British navy ordered 100 000 pulley-blocks a year. These machines were used for over 100 years.

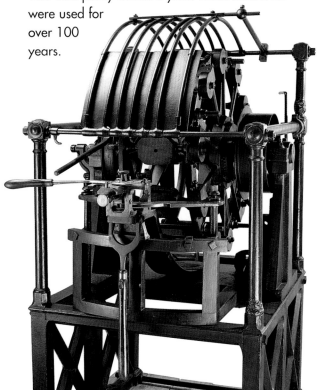

A brilliant failure

One of Isambard's most amazing projects was an 'atmospheric' railway that used air instead of locomotives to pull the train along. A pipe was laid between the rails, and rods connected pistons inside the pipe to the wagons of the train. Steam stations along the route removed air from the pipe, causing the pistons, and the train, to move forward. Strips of leather were used to make the joins in the pipe airtight, but these proved to be a big problem. They froze solid in winter and were constantly being eaten away by rats. Brunel built his atmospheric railway between Exeter and Newton Abbot in Devon in 1847, but it closed in less than a year.

A technical triumph

In 1825 Brunel began digging a tunnel under the River Thames. This was the first tunnel ever to be built under a river. It was difficult and dangerous. Workmen were protected by a tunnelling-shield Brunel designed but water kept pouring in, causing delays. Money ran out and work stopped for seven years. When the tunnel was finished, Brunel was knighted for his achievement. His tunnel was an engineering success but a commercial failure. For lack of money, the approach roads were never built so it could not carry traffic as intended. The strain of finishing the tunnel affected Marc Brunel's health and he died an invalid in 1849, aged 80.

The bridge the Brunels never saw

Isambard Brunel's daring design for the Clifton suspension bridge across the Avon Gorge at Bristol was chosen in preference to many others, including one by Thomas Telford. Money had been left for the project back in 1753 but engineering was not sufficiently advanced for it to be built until Brunel's day. Money problems meant that it was not finished until 1864, five years after Isambard's death and over 30 years after he had designed it. At 214m long and 79m high, it was the world's longest and highest suspension bridge at the time.

The Brunels' tunnel became one of London's major tourist attractions. Today, it carries a section of London's Underground railway.

A thorough training

Marc Brunel ensured that Isambard was properly trained as an engineer. There were no engineering courses at university in those days, so Isambard was sent to a top college in France to learn mathematics and to the London workshops of the engineer Henry Maudslay to learn practical skills. When he was 19, Isambard Brunel was put in charge of digging his father's tunnel beneath the Thames.

Constructing railways

Isambard's career began with building docks at Bristol. In 1833 he was appointed the engineer in charge of constructing the Great Western Railway from London to Bristol. The brick bridge he built for it at Maidenhead had the flattest arch in the world; the tunnel he engineered at Box, near Bath, was 3 km long. Isambard built over 1600 km of railways in England, Wales, Ireland and Italy, and he advised on many others in India and Australia.

Huge steamships

Isambard Brunel built three steamships, each of which, at launching, was the biggest ever built. The *Great Western* (1837), a wooden paddle-steamer, was the first steamship to provide a regular service across the Atlantic Ocean. The iron-hulled *Great Britain* (1843) was the first ever steamer driven by a **screw propeller**. It continued in service for 30 years, carrying troops out to the Crimean War and emigrants to the USA and Australia. In the end, it was beached in the Falkland Islands and used as a coal store. The *Great Britain* was rescued in 1970 and brought back to Britain for restoration. It can now be visited in the Bristol dock where it was built.

Powered by both sail and steam, the *Great Western's* first trip to New York took just 15 days. For ships powered by sail alone, the journey took over a month.

The *Great Eastern*

The 20 000-ton *Great Eastern* (1858) was so huge that it was launched sideways. It was intended to open up a new regular route to Asia and Australia but was too expensive to run. The construction of the ship caused Isambard Brunel many problems. In 1859, a few months after the launch, he collapsed and died shortly afterwards.

The *Great Eastern* was a triumph of engineering but it failed to make money for any of its owners. It was 211m long – no larger ship was built until 1899.

THOMAS EDISON

1847–1931

With only three months of formal education, Thomas Edison became one of the greatest inventors in history, who took out over 1000 patents in his lifetime.

Thomas Edison attended school for just three months of his life. His mother was a teacher who gave him some home tuition. By the time he was 15, he had learned Morse code so that he could operate an electric **telegraph**. While working as a telegrapher, Edison educated himself by reading and doing his own scientific experiments. He was influenced by the British scientist Michael Faraday's book *Experimental Researches in Electricity*, which taught him how to solve technical problems methodically.

Faster telegraphy

Edison's first inventions used telegraphy. One was an improved stock ticker, an electrical machine that transmitted price changes to businessmen in different cities. Edison designed one that printed letters as well as figures and soon had a factory making office equipment. Then, to quadruple the capacity of telegraph systems, he invented a way of sending two messages down a wire from each end at the same time.

A childhood accident left Edison permanently deaf. He claimed this made it easier for him to concentrate on his work.

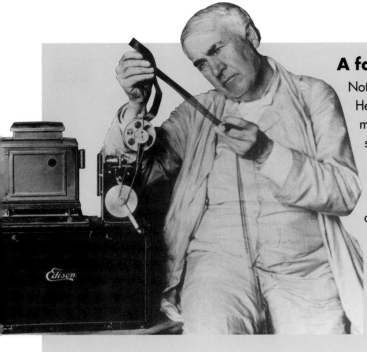

A far-sighted failure

Not all of Edison's inventions were successful. He spent thousands of dollars trying to make a film camera that would produce sound as well as pictures. Eventually he gave up, but he was sure that one day such machines would be found in every school: 'A large part of education in coming generations will not be by books but by moving pictures . . . Children don't need many books when they are shown how to do things. They can learn more by some kinds of moving pictures in five minutes than they can by the usual kinds of books in five hours.'

Inventing full time

By 1876 Edison had made enough money to give up manufacturing and devote himself to inventing full time. He set up what he called an 'invention factory' at Menlo Park, New Jersey, about 40 km from New York on the main railway line to Philadelphia. Here, Edison gathered a team of all sorts of skilled craftsmen, from woodworkers to watchmakers. When he became absorbed in a particular problem, he would often work at it until he fell asleep at his workbench and continue when he woke up, only returning home to eat and change his clothes. Edison once said, 'I owe my success to the fact that I never had a clock in my workroom.'

Edison's workrooms at Menlo Park were rebuilt at Henry Ford's Museum as a lasting tribute to one of America's greatest inventors.

First recorded sound

Edison's motto was 'never invent something people don't want'. The point was to find out what people needed and then invent it. But Edison did not always realise the potential of his inventions. In 1877 he invented the world's first machine for recording and playing back sound – the phonograph.

Edison testing his phonograph, the first ever device for recording sound.

The first words ever recorded were 'Mary had a little lamb.' Edison thought that busy people like himself could use it to record letters that could be typed up for them. He never imagined that it might be used to record music – but he did claim that it was his favourite invention.

An American hero

Edison believed in hard work. He used to say 'Genius is one per cent inspiration and 99 per cent perspiration.' In 1928, in recognition of a lifetime of achievement, the US Congress ordered a special gold medal to be struck in Edison's honour (he is seen here with his wife at the ceremony). A year later, a postage stamp was issued to celebrate the fiftieth anniversary of electric lighting.

Edison systematically tried hundreds of different materials before discovering the right one to make the filament for his light bulb.

New laboratory

In 1886 Edison built a new research centre at West Orange, New Jersey. This centre was bigger and better equipped than Menlo Park. He liked to plough back the money that he made from his inventions to work on new ideas. Edison wanted his inventions to make life easier and more enjoyable for ordinary people.

A new source of income

In 1898 rock suitable for making **cement** was found near Edison's home. He set up a cement works because he saw that people would like to travel on smooth cement roads rather than dirt tracks. He also foresaw that cement would be used to build cheaper homes. Edison's cement works became the fifth largest in the USA.

Workaholic

Edison was still working between 12 and 16 hours a day when he was in his seventies. He left behind him 3400 notebooks crammed with ideas. In 1929 Edison began to suffer from ill-health and spent less time in his laboratory. He died in 1931, aged 84.

Let there be light

In 1878 Edison invented the electric light bulb. An Englishman called Joseph Swan had actually demonstrated one already but Edison's was better. Instead of quarrelling about who should have the right to manufacture light bulbs, the two men agreed to work together as partners. Edison then designed the world's first electric power station so that whole towns could be lit with light bulbs. By 1883 Edison had set up lighting companies in France, Britain, Holland, Belgium, Italy, Germany and Russia. Edison said, 'I will make the electric light so cheap that only the rich will be able to burn candles.'

HENRY FORD

1863–1947

Both a technological genius and a brilliant businessman, Henry Ford did not invent the motor car, but he did invent a way of making them faster and cheaper than ever before.

Henry Ford was the son of a Michigan farmer, who left Ireland during the potato famine of the 1840s. From an early age he showed a dislike of farming and an interest in mechanics. His first experience of engineering came from mending farm tools. He left the farm at 16 to work as a machinist, then he made boat engines and worked in an electric company in Detroit. In 1891 he was offered a job as an engineer at the Detroit Edison Company. Two years later he was promoted to chief engineer.

Motor cars for the rich

By the early 1900s there were dozens of firms making cars but only very wealthy people could afford them. Most cars were built to order for each customer and took over a year to build. Even so, they were often unreliable. Many people employed a chauffeur to drive for them and when the car broke down, the chauffeur was required to repair it.

Unlike many engineers, Henry Ford had the financial skills to run a giant business. His River Rouge car plant was the world's largest factory, employing 81 000 workers in 1930.

The birth of motoring

The motor car was invented in Germany in 1885, when Gottlieb Daimler road-tested a massive home-made bicycle powered by a petrol engine. A few weeks later, Karl Benz produced the first petrol-engined road vehicle, which reached a speed of 13 km/h. This picture shows Benz with his wife in the first four-wheeled vehicle in 1893. Motor vehicles developed rapidly in France and Germany for military purposes, because each country feared the other would declare war on them.

Motor cars for everyone

Ford became very interested in cars and in 1893 he built a petrol engine. He imagined a world in which ordinary people would be able to afford a motor car, making their lives easier and more pleasurable. In 1896 he built a complete car, and in 1903 he founded the Ford Motor Company.

Standard parts

In 1905 Ford helped to found the Society of Automotive Engineers so that basic parts for motor vehicles could be made to standard sizes and patterns, and thus be interchangeable. This idea fitted well with his belief that 'the way to make automobiles is . . . to make them all alike.'

Ford's first vehicle, the Quadricycle, was steered with a tiller like a boat and had two forward speeds but no reverse.

Ford's fortune

By the 1920s the Ford business empire controlled its own fleet of ships, 16 coal mines, rubber plantations in Brazil and forests in Minnesota. Ford used his huge fortune to found two museums. In 1936 he and his son Edsel set up the Ford Foundation, which became the richest private foundation in the world with assets of $4 billion. It continues to support scientific research, education and charity.

Record breaking

From 1901 onwards, Ford made and drove his own racing cars. Building racing cars helped to publicise the Ford name – they also enabled him to try out new ideas in car design that could be adapted to ordinary cars. In 1904 he set a new world record by driving one of his own cars for a mile (1.6 km) in 39.4 seconds.

Cutting costs

Like all other cars, the first cars Ford made were expensive. Most cost around $1400. Ford wanted to make one to sell for $500. He believed that if he could find a way of making cars much cheaper, millions of people would want to buy them.

The Model T had to be tough as most roads outside cities had only a dirt surface.

The Model T

At that time, half the people in America lived on farms, just as Ford had as a boy. Every week they needed to go to the nearest town to shop and do business. They also needed transport to go to church or visit their neighbours. But a car for farmers would have to be tough and easy to fix if it went wrong, as well as cheap. In 1908 Ford designed the Model T, which sold for $850 – the right kind of car but still too costly.

Speedy manufacture

Cars were built by small teams of highly skilled craftsmen. Many used the system of fitting together **standardised** parts. In 1912 Ford combined this with the idea of organising his workers into one team that stretched out in a long line. Each worker added a part until a completed car came off the end of the production line. In this way, Ford workers could build cars eight times faster than before. Instead of buying parts from outside suppliers, the Ford company began to make its own. It also produced its own glass and steel. By 1914 Ford workers were able to produce a complete car in 93 minutes.

Delivery of parts to the worker by conveyor belt was timed to keep the assembly line moving smoothly and efficiently.

Well-paid workers

In 1914 Ford raised wages so that his workers were paid twice as much as the average worker in the car industry – $5 a day, instead of $2.34. Later, Ford raised the basic wage to $10, which meant that thousands of his own workers could afford to buy a Ford car. In this way, Ford used his own wage bill to expand the market for his output. He also cut the working day from nine hours to eight, gave his workers a share in company profits and built a special hospital to take care of them and their families. But he did not allow them to join **trade unions** until he was forced to by a strike in 1941.

Goodbye Model T

Ford cut the price of the Model T to $500 by 1913 and to $390 by 1915. By 1919 half of all the cars in the world were Model T Fords. Because of their lightweight bodywork they were known as 'Tin Lizzies'. In 1925 the price of the Model T dropped to $250. By the time Ford stopped making Model Ts in 1927, over 15 million had been produced. In 1928 he produced the Model A. It was available in four colours, 17 body styles and was the first to have safety glass. Ford businesses were at work in 33 countries, all financed from the profits of the original business. In 1947, a hundred years after his father left Ireland for a better life, Henry Ford died at the age of 83.

THE WRIGHT BROTHERS

Wilbur Wright 1867–1912
Orville Wright 1871–1948

The Wright brothers invented the first successful powered aircraft. But it was five years before their triumph had any practical effect.

The Wright brothers grew up in a large family in the American Midwest. Unlike their brothers and sisters, neither Wilbur nor Orville went to college. Instead, they set up a printing business and were soon making printing presses. Their interest in mechanical objects led them to open up another business, first selling and then making bicycles. Through these ventures they became skilled in making lightweight, precision machines of metal, wood and wire. The profits from their businesses helped them to finance their experiments.

First flights

Leonardo da Vinci (see page 13) had designed flying machines 400 years before the Wrights' experiments with powered flight, but his theories were never put into practice. In 1783 the first manned flight was in a hot air balloon made by the Montgolfier brothers. Further experiments at flying continued throughout the next century. These early efforts at flying made clear the problems: how to power a flying machine, how to steer it and how to land safely.

Wilbur (top) and Orville Wright did what other men and women of their time had only dreamed of – they flew.

Early gliders

The Wright brothers had heard of the experiments with gliders made by a German scientist, Otto Lilienthal. In 1896 he was killed flying one of his gliders, when it went out of control. The brothers were determined to carry on his work despite the danger and they read everything they could find about the infant science of **aeronautics**, including Sir George Cayley's work on the design of glider wings. They began to experiment with a double-winged kite to learn how a flying machine could best be controlled.

The ideal place

With the advice of the US Weather Bureau, the Wright brothers chose to carry out their experiments far from their Ohio home – at Kitty Hawk on the coast of North Carolina. It was suitably windy, had tall dunes from which to glide and soft sand on which to land.

German experimenter, Otto Lilienthal, made over 2000 glider flights before he was killed. His work provided the Wright brothers with valuable technical information about wing design.

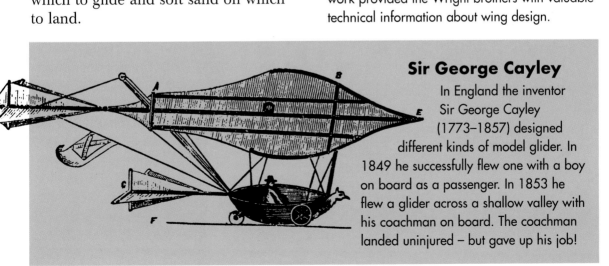

Sir George Cayley

In England the inventor Sir George Cayley (1773–1857) designed different kinds of model glider. In 1849 he successfully flew one with a boy on board as a passenger. In 1853 he flew a glider across a shallow valley with his coachman on board. The coachman landed uninjured – but gave up his job!

Determined to fly

The Wright brothers tried their first experimental glider in 1900 with Wilbur acting as pilot. The results were disappointing, so the following year they tried another version with wings that were almost twice as big. In this machine Wilbur managed to glide for 120m. To test out over 100 different shapes and size of wing, the brothers built a small wind tunnel. This helped them design their third full-scale glider. In 1902 both brothers piloted the glider, achieving flights of over 200m and staying airborne for up to 26 seconds.

Making history

Having spent another year perfecting a light, petrol-driven engine, the Wright brothers made their first powered flight on 17 December 1903. With Orville at the controls, *Flyer* covered 36m in 12 seconds. The brothers took turns to make three more flights that day. The fourth flight, piloted by Wilbur, lasted 59 seconds and covered 260m. In 1904 and 1905 they built two more planes.

Protecting their invention

Although they had been working on powered flight for almost 10 years, their success was known only to a few friends. The world at large was unaware that the Wright brothers had already made history. Fearing that their *Flyer* might be copied by rivals, the Wrights stopped further experiments while they took out a patent to protect their invention. This was granted in 1906.

The Wrights' *Flyer* was a biplane. There was no cockpit – the pilot lay in a cradle on the lower wing.

Flying over frontiers

Early in 1909, just five years after the Wrights' first flight, the *Daily Mail* newspaper offered a prize of £1000 to the first person to fly across the English Channel. It was won by a Frenchman, Louis Blériot (left). On the morning of 25 July 1909, he flew from Calais to Dover, where he crash-landed, unharmed, in a field near Dover Castle. The flight had taken him 37 minutes.

The future of flight

In 1908 the Wrights agreed to build a plane for the US Army that could carry a pilot and passenger for at least one hour at a speed of 65 km/h. In fact, the machine they delivered in 1909 went even faster and flew on its demonstration flight for 1 hour 12 minutes. By then, Orville had demonstrated one of their planes in France, Italy and Germany. In October 1909 Orville wrote, 'I firmly believe in the future of the aeroplane for commerce, to carry mail, to carry passengers . . . I cannot but believe that we stand at the beginning of a new era, the Age of Flight.' In the same month he set a new speed record of 112 km/h.

Historic honour

Wilbur Wright died in 1912, exhausted by overwork and weakened by typhoid. Orville sold his interest in their aircraft company in 1915 but continued to advise on designs. He remained interested in aviation research until his death in 1948. To mark the twenty-fifth anniversary of their first flight, the foundation stone of a monument was laid at Kitty Hawk in 1928. Completed in 1932, it was inscribed: 'In commemoration of the conquest of the air by the brothers Wilbur and Orville Wright. Conceived by genius. Achieved by dauntless resolution and unconquerable faith.'

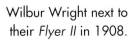

Wilbur Wright next to their *Flyer II* in 1908.

GLOSSARY

Aeronautics   The study of flight.

Amateur   Not trained.

Anatomy   The study of human or animal bodies.

Aqueduct   Bridge used as a channel for carrying water.

Architecture   The art of designing buildings.

Armoury   Factory for making weapons.

Astronomy   The study of the stars and planets.

Automotive   To do with motor vehicles.

Axle   Shaft on which a wheel turns.

Boring   Grinding a hole in something.

Botany   The study of plants.

Brewery   Factory that makes beer.

Bristle   Stiff animal hair.

Canal   Artificial waterway.

Cast   Make out of molten metal.

Cement   Powder mixed with sand and water to make concrete.

Civil engineering   Branch of engineering that includes building roads, dams, drains and power systems.

Cylinder   Tube shape.

Eclipse   Blocking out of Sun or Moon.

Estuary   Mouth of a river, where it meets the sea.

Fibre   Thread.

Fortifications   Defences.

Gear   Toothed wheel that connects with another toothed wheel to transmit power in a machine.

Geometry   Branch of mathematics concerned with shapes, surfaces and solids.

Interchangeable   Able to be swapped around.

Lever   Bar for lifting or moving objects.

Loch   Scottish word for lake.

Marine engineering   Branch of engineering dealing with ships' engines and equipment.

Mass production Making identical objects on a large scale.

Mechanical engineering Branch of engineering dealing with machines.

Milling machine Machine for cutting or shaping metal.

Musket Gun with a long barrel.

Navigational instruments Devices for finding directions at sea.

Patent Legal agreement giving people the sole rights to their inventions – no one can copy the invention without the inventor's permission.

Plantation Farm with large areas given over to one crop, for example, sugar or bananas.

Pneumatic Air-powered.

Professional Trained to do a particular job for a living.

Roller Cylinder used to flatten things.

Rotary Going round and round.

Screw propeller Rotary shaft with spiral blades to drive a ship.

Sculptor Artist who carves or makes statues

Shift The arrangement of hours in a working day.

Standardised Made to a set pattern.

Stone mason Craftsman trained to cut and build with stone.

Surveyor Person skilled in measuring land.

Suspension bridge Bridge hung from cables that are anchored by towers.

Telegraph System by which information is carried over long distances using coded electrical signals.

Trade union An association of workers formed to improve their wages and working conditions.

Turbine Powerful steam engine driving rotary blades to power a ship or make electricity.

Valve Flap or tap to control a flow of liquid or gas.

Vending machine Machine for selling goods.

Wagonway Rail track along which wagons are pulled.

Watermill Mill powered by flowing water.

INDEX

aeolipile 8
aeronautics 43
aircraft 42, 45
amateur 22,
aqueduct 4, 23
armoury 20
axle 11

Benz, Karl 39
biplane 44
Blériot, Louis 45
Borgia, Cesare 12
Boulton, Matthew 15, 17
bridge 4, 5, 22, 23, 24
  25, 26, 29, 32
bristles 19
Britannia Bridge 25
Brunel, Isambard
  Kingdom 5, 29,
  30–33
Brunel, Marc Isambard
  5, 30–32

Caledonian Canal 15,
  24
canal 5, 12, 22, 23, 24
catapult 11
Catch Me Who Can
27
Cayley, Sir George 43
cement 37
civil engineering 5
Colt, Samuel 21
cotton 16, 18, 21, 27
cotton gin 19, 20

Daimler, Gottlieb 39

Edison, Thomas 5,
  34–37
Ellesmere Canal
  Company 24

fibre 18
Flyer 44
flying 42, 44, 45
Ford, Henry 5, 38–41
Ford Motor Company 39

fortifications 11, 12
freight 27

gears 9
geometry 10
glider 43, 44
Great Britain 33
Great Eastern 33
Great Western 33
Gota Canal 24

helicopter 5, 13
Hero of Alexandria 4,
  6–9
High Level Bridge 29
horsepower 17
hot air balloon 42

Industrial Revolution 5
Institution of Civil
  Engineers 25
Institution of Mechanical
  Engineers 28
interchangeable parts
  20, 39

Killingworth Colliery 28
Kitty Hawk 43, 45

Leonardo da Vinci 5,
  10–13, 42
lever 11
light bulb 37
Lilienthal, Otto 43
Liverpool and Manchester
  line 27
loch 24
locomotive 5, 16, 26,
  27, 28, 31
Lunar Society 17

marine engineering 5
mass production 30
mechanical engineering
  5
Menai Bridge 25
Menlo Park 35, 37
Metrica 7

milling machine 20
mine 15
mirror writing 13
Model A 41
Model T 40, 41
Mona Lisa 11
Montgolfier brothers 42
motor car 38–41
movie camera 35
musket 20, 21

Newcomen engine 14,
  15
Newcomen, Thomas 14
notebooks 12,

paddle-steamer 33
painter 10
passenger 27, 45
patent 14, 19, 20, 34,
  44
petrol engine 35, 44
phonograph 36
pilot 44, 45
pneumatic power 9
power station 37
printing press 9, 16, 42
production line 41
professional 22, 25
pulley 11
pulley-block 30, 31

quadricycle 39

railway 4, 5, 26, 27,
  28, 29, 31
revolver 21
River Rouge car plant 38
road 4, 5, 7, 22, 23,
  25, 31
Rocket 27
rollers 18
rotary engine 16
Royal Society 17

Savery, Thomas 14
science 4, 11, 12, 43
screw propeller 33

sculptor 10
Society of Automotive
  Engineers 39
sound 35, 36
standard gauge 28
standardised parts 41
steam engine 4. 6, 8,
  14,
steam power 16, 21,
steamships 5, 33
Stephenson, George 5,
  26–28
Stephenson, Robert 25,
  26–29
stock ticker 34
Stockton and Darlington
  line 27
stone mason 22
surveyor 15, 23
suspension bridge 25,
  32
Swan, Joseph, 41

telegraphy 34
Telford, Thomas 5,
  22–25, 29, 32
Thames tunnel 31, 32
'Tin Lizzie' 41
Trevithick, Richard 27,
  28
tunnelling-shield 31

valve 9
vending machine 9

wagonway 28
water clock 7, 9
watt 17
Watt, James 14–17
weapons 7, 10
West Orange 41
Whitney, Eli 18–21
Whitney, Eli Jr. 21
wind tunnel 44
wings 43, 44
Wright, Orville 42–45
Wright, Wilbur 42–45